S0-BID-213

# Today
# In Old New York

Text By ElvaJean Hall & Beatrice H. Criner
Sketches by Lois Axeman

72604

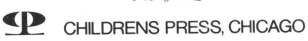

CHILDRENS PRESS, CHICAGO

THE NYACK LIBRARY
NYACK, N. Y. 10960

# INTRODUCTION

New York has changed so much since the American Revolution that you will be surprised to find so many reminders of the colonial city among the skyscrapers . . .

You can see where the first Dutch settlers built a fort to guard the city.

You can stand where patriots stood to hear the Declaration of Independence for the first time, where they set up a Liberty pole and made a valiant last stand.

More than any other person, you will find reminders of George Washington here— where he slept and worked, where he said goodbye to his officers. You can sit in his pew in St. Paul's Chapel and see where he was sworn in as the new country's first President.

Copyright© 1975 by Regensteiner Publishing Enterprises, Inc. All rights reserved. Published simultaneously in Canada. Printed in the United States of America.

Today in Old New York
Created by T.A. Chacharon & Associates, Ltd.

**Library of Congress Cataloging in Publication Data**
Hall, Elvajean.
　　　Today in old New York.
　　　SUMMARY: Explains in simple text and illustrations the historical significance of New York City's most important historic buildings and sights.
　　　1. New York (City) History—Colonial period, ca. 1600-1775—Juvenile literature. 2. New York (City)—History—Revolution, 1775-1783—Juvenile literature. (1. New York (City)—History—Colonial period, ca. 1600-1775. 2. New York (City)—History—Revolution, 1775-1783) I. Criner, Beatrice H., 1915-　　　joint author. II. Axeman, Lois. III. Title.
F128.4.H37　　　974.7'1　　　75-20422
ISBN O-516-03813-3

Photographs courtesy of the New York Convention & Visitors Bureau
Front Cover View—Sniffer Court

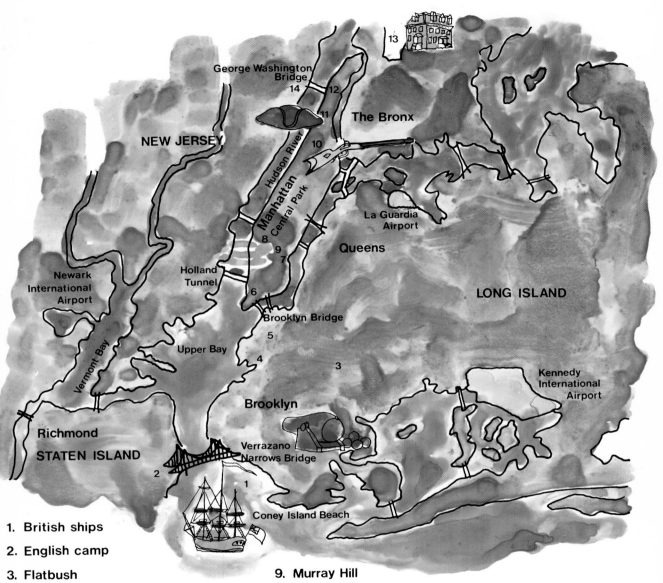

1. British ships

2. English camp

3. Flatbush

4. Gowanus Creek

5. American fort on Brooklyn Heights

6. New York

7. Kip's Bay

8. Washington stops fleeing troops

9. Murray Hill

10. Harlem Heights

11. Washington's headquarters

12. Fort Washington

13. Van Cortlandt mansion & burial vault

14. Fort Lee (New Jersey)

## BATTERY PARK

Battery Park is a good place to begin looking at old New York. It is where New York actually began.

If you stand in Battery Park and look out at the water, you can see why people would choose this spot for a town.

There is a sheltered harbor where several rivers meet. One river, the Hudson, runs far inland. A fort built here could defend the harbor and rivers.

One plaque you will see in Battery Park marks the original Fort Amsterdam.

In 1626 a group of Dutch settlers led by Peter Minuit arrived here. He bought Manhattan Island from the Indians and built a fort.

The Dutch were not the first Europeans to find this fine harbor.

Probably the first was an explorer named Giuseppe da Verrazano. He sailed into the harbor in 1524. A statue of Verrazano stands in Battery Park. The huge new bridge across the Narrows is named for him, too.

But the Dutch were the first to settle here. They built a town like those at home. They named it New Amsterdam.

It had small brick houses and narrow, crooked streets. The streets of lower Manhattan today still twist and wind as the streets of New Amsterdam did.

You can still find reminders of New Amsterdam in New York today. Many names tell you about the city's past.

One of the Dutch governors was a peppery, peg-legged man named Peter Stuyvesant. He worried about the Indians whose villages were scattered over Manhattan Island.

So at the northern edge of the town, he built a wooden wall to defend it. That is where Wall Street is today.

After New Amsterdam, the Dutch built another town further north. They called it New Haarlem, after a town in Holland.

A winding road ran the length of the island to connect the towns. It was called the Broad Way. Today Broadway still runs the length of Manhattan.

Peter Stuyvesant chose for his farm
some rich land northeast of the settlement.
Today Stuyvesant Square and the houses
of Stuyvesant Town stand on this land.

Stuyvesant also built a chapel and
a road leading to town. In Dutch,
a farm is a *bouwerie*. Stuyvesant's road
was the first Bowery.

He is buried in the grounds of his
chapel, called St. Mark's-in-the-Bouwerie.

The Dutch built other towns, across
the river. Jacob Bronck's land is now
the Bronx. And the hilly "broken land"
is now called Brooklyn.

In 1664 the English took over this land
from the Dutch. They renamed the fort at
the Battery Fort James, after the king.
They renamed the town New York.

By the time of the Revolution, New York
had grown a few miles north of Wall Street.
About 20,000 people lived there.

Many of the forests had been cleared
to make fine farms and apple orchards.

There were still brick houses and
narrow streets and open meadows in the town.
Some New Yorkers rented a small field
just north of the Battery. It became the
Bowling Green, where they practiced their
favorite sport, lawn bowling.

## CITY HALL PARK — "THE FIELDS"

The heart of every colonial city was
its "common." The common land belonged
to everyone in the city.

Sometimes sheep and cows grazed there.
Sometimes the militia paraded there.
Sometimes there were public meetings.

In New York the common was known as
The Fields. In 1776 they were near the
northern limits of the city. Today they
are downtown, in City Hall Park.

New York's City Hall was built here
about twenty years after the Revolution.

The New York colonists were never
peaceful subjects of Britain. One royal
governor after another came and failed.

New Yorkers objected to the taxes
that Britain put on many things.

They also resented having to provide
food and housing for British soldiers.
The largest group of soldiers in America was
in New York.

The English law that caused the most
trouble in the colonies was the Stamp Act
of 1765. It required every important
paper — even newspapers — to carry a
special tax stamp.

In New York, people made angry speeches against the Stamp Act. One man shouted that the Americans were "sons of liberty."

A secret group that had been fighting the tax laws took this as its name.

Angry delegates came to New York for a special Congress to talk about the Stamp Act. Merchants agreed not to trade with England until the act was repealed.

But the Sons of Liberty wanted action, not meetings. They built a gallows in The Fields and hanged dummies that looked like the British officials. They took the governor's carriage and burned it.

The next year, England repealed the
Stamp Act. The Sons of Liberty led a
victory celebration in The Fields. There
were bands, cannon, bonfires, and beer.

Next they put up a Liberty pole. It
was a tall sapling with a liberty cap on top.

The British soldiers thought the
Liberty poles were an insult to the king.
Every so often they would cut one down,
and there would be a fight.

The worst of these was the Battle of
Golden Hill in January 1770. Soldiers with
bayonets fought patriots with clubs. Several
people were seriously hurt.

Finally the radical Sons of Liberty
got together with more level-headed New
Yorkers. They put up a pole inscribed "Liberty
and Property" in The Fields. The British
let this one stand.

But rebellion in the colonies was growing
steadily stronger. The colonists protested
every tax that Parliament passed.

Delegates went to the Continental
Congresses in Philadelphia. In 1775 they named
George Washington commander of a
Continental Army to fight for their rights.

Early in 1776 a special Congress met.
On July 4, 1776, it approved the newly written
Declaration of Independence.

When the news reached New York on
July 9, Washington called together his troops.
They marched to The Fields and stood at
attention while an officer read the Declaration
aloud.

Many New Yorkers wanted just their
rights — not independence. But the Declaration
was wildly cheered and approved.

Perhaps one reason was that even before
the message of independence arrived,
thousands of British troops were gathering
near New York.

On July 2, General William Howe had landed about 10,000 British soldiers on Staten Island. The crowd in The Fields celebrating independence could see the masts of British ships in the harbor.

After the Declaration was read, the soldiers and the Sons of Liberty went wild.

They rushed downtown to the statue of King George that stood in the Bowling Green. Knocking the statue over, they broke off its head.

They knew that now they would have to fight a war for independence. Soon the metal in the king's statue would be melted into bullets for the Continental Army.

## THE MORRIS-JUMEL MANSION

North of the colonial city of New York
were rugged, rolling woods and farmlands.
Many wealthy New Yorkers had large farms
with beautiful manor houses.

Roger Morris had built his fine house
on a hill with a beautiful view. But Morris
was a Loyalist. He fled to London when war
broke out.

When Washington's army fortified
Manhattan, the general took the Morris house
for his New York headquarters.

After the retreat from Long Island
and the unsuccessful peace conference,
Washington knew he could not hold New York.

He sent his troops north to the defenses
at Harlem Heights.

While the army was moving, Washington
sat at a desk in the Morris house. He
puzzled over maps of the American defenses
and British soldiers and ships.

Suddenly he heard the sound of cannon.
He rushed out, followed by his officers.
Jumping on his horse, Washington galloped
toward the sound.

The British were landing on Manhattan!

General Howe's troops had crossed the
East River to the landing at Kip's Bay,
about where 34th Street is today.

A small group of American militia was
guarding the landing. But they were young,
untrained soldiers. The cannon fire and
the British troops terrified them.

When Washington arrived, he found
his troops running away.

General Washington had a temper. Now he
was both angry and discouraged.

"Are these the men I am supposed to
defend America with?" he shouted.

He tried to rally the troops, but soon
only he and his officers were left facing
the British troops. They had been driven
back from the river to about where
Bryant Park is today.

The tall, angry general sat stubbornly
on his big horse, refusing to retreat.

At last a young officer grabbed the
horse's bridle and pulled Washington out
of danger.

If he had been killed or captured, the
Revolution might have ended right there.

Only half the American army managed
to reach Harlem Heights before the British
attack. General Putnam and General Knox,
with most of the American cannon, were
trapped at the Battery, the southern tip of
the island.

Twelve miles of rugged country lay between
the two parts of the American army.

If the British moved quickly across
Manhattan, they would split the army in two.

The British began to move up the post
road toward Harlem. They marched about where
Fifth Avenue is today.

Down at the Battery, the Americans were
worried and frightened. Then General Putnam's
young aide, Aaron Burr, spoke up.

"I used to go hunting here," he said.
"I know ways to cross the island that the
British will never find."

Burr led the troops through the hills and
forests at the edge of the island, west of
what is now Central Park. Though they were
only about a mile from the British, thick
woods lay between them.

The tired Americans ran quickly and quietly,
climbing over rocks and dodging trees.

While the Americans rushed north in panic, General Howe was taking his time.

That afternoon he and his officers reached the pleasant farm of Robert Murray. (That section of the city is still called Murray Hill.)

Mary Lindley Murray invited the general to stop and have tea. The British officers relaxed in the shade for a few hours.

Only a few miles away, Aaron Burr was leading the American troops to safety at Harlem Heights. Most people think now that Mrs. Murray planned her tea party just to delay the comfort-loving General Howe.

## THE PEACE CONFERENCE HOUSE

Although most of the colonial buildings
in New York City are gone, many houses still
stand on Staten Island, across the bay.

When General Howe decided to invade
New York, he landed his troops on
Staten Island. They camped near where the
Verrazano-Narrows Bridge now ends.

From Staten Island, Howe could block
American ships from leaving New York harbor.

He made his headquarters in this house
in Tottenville. It belonged to a Loyalist
named Billopp.

Many Englishmen had a lot of sympathy for the colonists. They agreed that perhaps the government had been unfair in passing laws like the Stamp Act.

Oddly, two of these sympathetic Englishmen were the commanders of the troops sent to America. One was General William Howe himself — nicknamed "Sir Billy." The other was his older brother, Lord Richard Howe. Lord Howe was admiral of the fleet.

Before the Howes left, King George gave them the power to seek peace.

By August 1776, there were about 32,000 British troops on Staten Island. They outnumbered the Americans by nearly two to one.

General Howe sent an offer of peace to General Washington — if the "rebels" would give in. Scornfully, Washington refused.

So Howe got ready to attack the defenses on Long Island. His men crossed the harbor by ferry. In the middle of the night, they attacked from three different directions.

Surprised and confused, the Americans retreated to the defenses on the bluffs of Brooklyn Heights.

Suddenly a storm broke. Their gunpowder was soaked. Neither army could fight.

Washington saw that the battle was hopeless. They were trapped.

"Reinforcements are coming," he told the men calmly. "March out of camp."

Hurriedly he sent a message to one regiment from Massachusetts.

In the dark and rainy night, the strong arms of the Massachusetts fishermen rowed all the Americans across the river to Manhattan.

Washington watched until the last small boat was safely away.

When the rain stopped the next morning, Howe was ready to attack. But the Americans were gone!

After this battle, the Howes thought
the Americans might be ready to give in.

Lord Howe asked the Congress to send
someone to discuss peace. Congress named
Benjamin Franklin, John Adams, and Edward
Rutledge.

On September 11, they met with Howe at
the Billopp house on Staten Island.

Everyone was polite and pleasant. But
Lord Howe asked for one thing the Americans
could not grant — they would have to take back
the Declaration of Independence.

No, said the Americans. Peace on those
terms was impossible.

The war would go on. The only peace
conference of the Revolution was over.

# FORT WASHINGTON

It may be hard to imagine that Manhattan was once a rugged wilderness, covered by thick forests. Only at the northern tip of the island can you see what it was like in Revolutionary days.

Here in Fort Tryon Park is the highest point on Manhattan, the crest of a rocky ridge. This is where the Americans made their last stand in Manhattan.

Fort Washington was a field fort. The retreating army built it in a hurry. Today the spot is marked by just a circle of stones and a flag.

After the attack at Kip's Bay,
Washington's soldiers had fled north to
the defenses at Harlem Heights, about
where Columbia University is today.

All the army was together again.
Now their courage came back. In a quick,
hard-fought battle at Harlem Heights,
they sent the British and Hessian
soldiers into retreat.

It was their first real military victory
of the Revolution.

General Washington waited in Harlem for the next British attack. He needed information—where would General Howe move? And when?

One of Washington's young officers had the information. Captain Nathan Hale had volunteered to get behind British lines. Disguised as a Dutch schoolmaster, he had found out their plans.

Hale was on his way back when the British stopped him. Many people think his own cousin, a Loyalist, gave him away.

The soldiers brought Nathan Hale to
General Howe's headquarters in the
Beekman House, near where the United Nations
now stands.

Hale had maps and plans. The British
held a quick trial in a greenhouse on the
estate. The next day, September 22, they
hanged him as a spy. He was only 21.

His courage so impressed one English
officer that he wrote down Hale's last
words: "I only regret that I have but
one life to give for my country."

Early in October, General Howe made his move. He sent troops by boat up the East River into Long Island Sound.

Washington saw danger coming. Howe could now easily surround him. Washington knew he could no longer defend Manhattan.

He left a strong force at Fort Washington. The rest of the army moved across the river to White Plains and to New Jersey.

The British liked to call Washington "the old fox," thinking they could capture him the way hunters catch a fox. During most of 1776, the fox kept slipping away.

Finally Howe stopped chasing Washington.

He concentrated on Fort Washington. On November 16, 13,000 troops attacked the 3,000 who held the river fort.

One of the defenders of Fort Washington was not a man, but a woman, Molly Corbin. Like many other soldiers' wives, she traveled with the army.

When a man was wounded, Molly and her husband fought side by side at the cannon. Then John Corbin was hit. Molly stayed at her post, loading and firing the cannon.

Finally, though, the fort fell. Manhattan was now all in British hands. It would remain there until the war ended, seven years later.

## FRAUNCES' TAVERN

The war seemed to end slowly. Two years had passed since the proud Lord Cornwallis had surrendered to Washington at Yorktown.

Now at last the peace treaty was signed. It was November 1783. And the British were leaving New York.

Seven years of occupation had been hard for New Yorkers. Two great fires had swept the city in 1776 and 1778. Many people had only tents to live in.

Silent crowds in the ruined city watched boatloads of redcoats being rowed out to the British ships.

Then Washington and his officers appeared.
They rode on horseback, two by two,
all the way to Fort George at the Battery.
The crowds wept and cheered.
The Union Jack over the fort was cut down.
The Stars and Stripes was raised once again
over New York.
Washington's job as commander of the
army was ended. He had only one more duty.
He must say goodbye to all the officers
who had served him so faithfully.

On December 4, 1783, they met in the
Long Room on the second floor of Fraunces'
Tavern, on the corner of Broad and Pearl streets.

This handsome building had once been a
private home. "Black Sam" Fraunces,
a West Indian, had made it into a popular
inn and hotel for New Yorkers.

One by one, the officers came to say
goodbye to their general. Washington was so
moved that he could only take their hands
silently.

But though he was sad to leave his men,
Washington was happy to be going back to
the life of a Virginia planter. He would
be home at Mount Vernon for Christmas for
the first time in eight years.

## ST. PAUL'S CHAPEL

The new United States would not let
George Washington retire to Mt. Vernon.
In April 1789, Washington returned to
New York. On the balcony of Federal Hall
on Wall Street, he was sworn in as
the first President under the Constitution.

Federal Hall was across the street from
where the Stock Exchange now stands. You
can still see a statue of Washington there.

The first presidential mansion in
New York was on Cherry Street. While
Washington lived here as President, he went to
church at St. Paul's, a few blocks north.

St. Paul's is the oldest church left in
Manhattan. Most of the others burned in
the great fire of September 1776.

But St. Paul's is the same elegant church
that New Yorkers were proud of in 1766.
Then its broad lawn sloped westward all
the way to the Hudson River.

Inside, the pews were painted white with
gold trim. You can still see the pew where
Washington sat when he worshipped here.

New York remained the capital of the
United States until 1800. Then a new city was
planned and named for George Washington.

## TIME LINE

| | |
|---|---|
| 1626 | Dutch buy Manhattan Island from Indians |
| 1664 | English take over New Amsterdam and rename it New York |
| 1765 | British Parliament passes Stamp Act |
| Jan. 18, 1770 | Battle of Golden Hill |
| July 2, 1776 | General Howe's troops land on Staten Island |
| July 9, 1776 | Declaration of Independence read in New York |
| Aug. 29 - 30, 1776 | Battle of Brooklyn Heights |
| Sept. 11, 1776 | Peace conference on Staten Island |
| Sept. 15, 1776 | British land at Kip's Bay and occupy New York |
| Sept. 21, 1776 | Great fire destroys much of New York |
| Sept. 22, 1776 | Nathan Hale hanged as American spy |
| Nov. 16, 1776 | Fort Washington falls to British |
| Nov. 21, 1783 | British troops leave New York |
| Dec. 4, 1783 | Washington says farewell to his officers |
| April 30, 1789 | Washington inaugurated as President |

# PLACES TO VISIT IN NEW YORK CITY

## HISTORICAL SITES

Dyckman House
Federal Hall National Monument
Hamilton Grange
Quaker Meetinghouse (Queens)
St. Marks-in-the-Bouwerie
Trinity Church
Van Cortlandt Mansion (Bronx)
Voorlezer's House (Staten Island)

## GENERAL INTEREST

Bronx Zoo
Brooklyn Bridge
The Cloisters
Empire State Building
Lincoln Center
Staten Island Ferry
Radio City Music Hall
Rockefeller Center
Statue of Liberty
Verrazano-Narrows Bridge
United Nations
World Trade Center

## MUSEUMS

American Museum of Natural History
Guggenheim Museum
Metropolitan Museum of Art
Museum of the American Indian
Museum of the City of New York
Museum of Modern Art
New York Historical Society
South St. Seaport Museum

## HOTELS and RESTAURANTS

Americana
New York Hilton
Plaza
St. Regis-Sheraton